UNSTOPPABLE

"Conquer every JEE/NEET challenge with focus, strength

and resilience"

N.B.V.SubbaRao

Printed in India.

Price : Rs 400/-

For more information, or to book an event,

contact : info@innovativeclasses.com

http://www.innovativeclasses.com

Second Edition : Feb-2025

Dedicated to

To all my wonderful students,

Your unwavering commitment and resilience

have taught me the depth of every struggle and

the true power of consistency. You inspire me

every day to believe in the strength of

perseverance and the beauty of learning through

challenges.

Content

Chapter 1:

The Silent Thieves of JEE/NEET Preparation

Chapter2:

Overcoming Comparison and Bias

Chapter 3:

From Frustration to Mastery - Overcoming Dislike of a Subject

CHAPTER4:

Reignite the Spark - The revision phase: The Hero's Journey

Chapter 5:

The Strength of Minor Victories - How Every Day Contributes to Your Achievement

Chapter6:

Overcoming Exam Hall Nerves: Converting Fear into Motivation for Achievement

Conclusion: The Journey Ahead – Your Future Awaits

Introduction

The journey of preparing for competitive exams like JEE/NEET/NEET is as much a test of character as it is of knowledge. Over the years, I have observed countless students with immense potential who, despite their capabilities, struggle to achieve their goals. Why? Often, the reasons lie not in a lack of intelligence or effort but in inconsistency, mental blocks, and unresolved emotional challenges. These issues, if not addressed, not only impact on their immediate results but can also linger for years, casting a shadow on their self-confidence and future endeavours.

I've worked closely with students and studied their challenges deeply. I've seen bright young minds burdened by procrastination, self-doubt, comparison, and the fear of failure. Their dreams dim not because they lack ability but because they lack guidance to navigate these mental and emotional hurdles. These experiences, documented over the years through real case studies, have shaped my understanding of the unique struggles students face during this crucial phase of their lives.

This Book is not just a guide; it's a companion for every JEE/NEET aspirant. It addresses the most common and overlooked challenges students face during preparation, offering practical solutions that are easy to implement. From battling procrastination to overcoming the fear of a subject, from handling preoccupied thoughts to finding focus in a noisy world—this book provides a structured path to help students regain control and unlock their true potential.

But this Book is about more than personal success. Every student preparing for JEE/NEET today is part of the foundation of **Vikasit Bharat,** a developed India. By empowering these young minds to overcome their struggles, we are contributing to a greater mission—building a future where these children lead with confidence, resilience, and excellence. This book is my humble contribution as an educator to this noble vision.

To all JEE/NEET aspirants reading this: know that you are not alone in your struggles. With the right mindset, strategies, and support, you can conquer any challenge that comes your way. Let this Book be your guide, and let your journey be a testament to your strength and determination. Together, let's build a brighter future—one success story at a time.

CHAPTER 1

The Silent Thieves of JEE/NEET/NEET Preparation

"From Delay to Discipline: Mastering the First Step"

Preparation for JEE/NEET isn't just about solving equations or memorizing concepts; it's about mastering your mindset and staying consistent in the face of challenges. But let's face it—there are days when getting started feels impossible, motivation runs dry, or distractions steal away precious hours. At times, self-doubt creeps in, monotony dulls your focus, and mental exhaustion makes every effort seem like an uphill battle. Add to this the chaos of preoccupied thoughts clouding your clarity, and it becomes clear why so many capable students struggle to stay on track.

This chapter is your roadmap to overcome these hurdles. Through practical strategies and actionable insights, it addresses one dozen key obstacles that hold students back:

1. **Procrastination**: Learn how to conquer the inertia that delays your progress and turn hesitation into action.

2. **Overwhelming Syllabus:** Too Much to Handle but Master the art of breaking down massive tasks into achievable goals and transforming

chaos into clarity for lifelong strength.

3. **Low Motivation**: Reignite your inner drive by reconnecting with your purpose and setting achievable micro-goals.

4. **Distractions**: Discover how to create a focus-friendly environment and outsmart the constant pull of social media and entertainment.

5. **Lack of Confidence**: Build unshakable self-belief by understanding your strengths and reframing failures as opportunities.

6. **Monotony**: Inject variety and excitement into your routine to keep your preparation fresh and engaging.

7. **Mental Exhaustion**: Recharge effectively with proven techniques that enhance your energy and mental stamina.

8. **Mental Clarity**: Clear the clutter in your mind and focus your thoughts with mindfulness and time-tested mental exercises.

9. **The "Plateau Phase" Struggle**: Stuck in a Rut- Learn to push through stagnation with renewed strategies and resilience, turning setbacks into steppingstones for lifelong growth.

10. **Sleep Deprivation: The Silent Saboteur** – Prioritize quality rest to recharge your mind and body, turning sleep into your ultimate performance enhancer.

11. **Comparing with Others: The Confidence Killer** – Embrace your unique journey, silencing self-doubt and building unshakable self-belief.

12. **Family Expectations: The Invisible Weight** – Transform the silent pressure of loved ones' hopes into a bond of shared dreams, fueled by understanding, trust, and heartfelt communication.

Through real-life examples, relatable metaphors, and expert-backed techniques, this chapter equips you with the tools to take control of your preparation. Each obstacle is an opportunity in disguise—your chance to rise stronger, smarter, and more determined. Let me remind you of a powerful story from the great epic **Shrimad Ramayana** that is most appropriate here.

The Struggles of a Journey: Lessons from **Shrimad Ramayana.**

In every great journey, obstacles test our resolve and determination. In the epic ***Shrimad Ramayana,*** Lord Rama's search for Sita was one of the most challenging phases of his life. The journey wasn't straightforward—there were moments of doubt, exhaustion, and setbacks. But through resilience, clarity of purpose, and the unwavering support of his Vanara allies, Lord Rama turned every challenge into an opportunity. His relentless spirit transformed the impossible into victory.

For students preparing for JEE/NEET, the journey is no less demanding. The path to success is filled with hurdles—procrastination, mental fatigue, fear of failure, and external pressures. Just like Lord Rama sought the guidance and support of trusted allies like Hanuman, you too need the right strategies and mindset to navigate this demanding phase of life.

When Lord Rama stood at the shores of the vast ocean, seeking a way to reach Lanka, it seemed like an insurmountable challenge. Yet, with determination, he built the bridge one step at a time, eventually achieving what seemed impossible.

The lesson is clear: every great journey, whether it's finding Sita or acing the JEE/NEET exams, begins with **clarity of purpose, consistent effort, and trust in your abilities**. Your bridge to success will be built not in a single leap but through steady, intentional actions.

By weaving Rama's story into your preparation, you'll not only find inspiration but also a reminder that struggles are an essential part of achieving greatness. Let this chapter be your guide to face each obstacle head-on and emerge victorious—not just in JEE/NEET but in life.

Now, let's dive deeper into the 12 key obstacles and how to tackle them, one by one. Your epic journey starts here. Remember, every great journey begins with a single step. But in practical, when self-preparation feels hard, students often face challenges that pull them away from productive work. Here's a tailored framework focusing on these challenges, with actionable strategies, and motivational stories to help aspirants stay on track:

1. Procrastination: The Silent Thief of Time

Challenge:

"I know I need to study, but I keep postponing it."

Story: The Rusty Bike

Imagine a bike left unused—it becomes rusty and difficult to ride. Similarly, procrastination makes starting tasks harder, but once you get going, the "rust" wears off, and the process becomes smoother.

Techniques:

1. **The 2-Minute Rule:**

   o Commit to studying for just 2 minutes. Often, starting is the hardest part, and once you begin, you're likely to continue.

2. **Accountability Partner:**

   o Pair up with a friend or sibling and share daily goals. Hold each other accountable for progress.

3. **Reward System:**

   o Promise yourself a small reward (e.g., your favourite snack or 10 minutes of relaxation) after completing a study session.

Case study:

My student Ramya kept procrastinating on revising Organic Chemistry. By starting with just 2-minute sessions, she overcame the inertia and eventually built a solid routine, mastering her weak subject.

2. Overwhelming Syllabus: Too Much to Handle

Challenge

"The syllabus feels endless. I don't know where to start or how to finish everything."

Story: Eating an Elephant

How do you eat an elephant? One bite at a time. The syllabus may seem gigantic but breaking it into smaller chunks makes it manageable.

Case study:

Ravi, a JEE/NEET aspirant, felt lost with the syllabus until he followed a 45-day plan focusing only on high-priority chapters. He didn't cover everything, but his strategic preparation got him an AIR under 1000 in JEE Mains.

Actionable Insight:

- **Chunking Strategy:** Divide your syllabus into daily and weekly goals. Prioritize topics with higher weightage.

- **Focus on the Now:** Avoid worrying about the entire syllabus. Concentrate only on what's scheduled for today.

3. Low Motivation: When the Goal Feels Distant

Challenge:

"I feel stuck, and my goals seem too far away."

Story: The Mountain and the Steps

Climbing a mountain seems overwhelming when you look at the peak. But focusing on each step makes the journey manageable and rewarding.

Techniques:

1. **Chunk Goals:**

   - Break large topics into smaller sections. For example, instead of "Revise Physics," set a goal like "Revise Newton's Laws for 1 hour."

2. **Daily Wins Journal:**

   o   Write down one thing you achieved each day, no matter how small. These wins remind you of your progress.

3. **Visualize Success:**

   o   Spend 5 minutes daily imagining yourself in your dream college or achieving your target score. This keeps your motivation alive.

4. Distractions: The Pull of Social Media and Entertainment

Challenge:

"I keep getting distracted by my phone, YouTube, or chatting with friends."

Story: The Leaking Bucket

A bucket with holes can never fill up, no matter how much water you pour in. Distractions are like those holes, draining your time and energy without letting you achieve your goals.

Techniques:

1. **Digital Detox:**

- o   Use apps like StayFocusd or Forest to block distracting websites and apps during study hours but it's better to away from all types of devices when you are in deep learning. Remember, no app can guide you better than self-realization.

2. **Dedicated Study Zone:**

- o   Create a distraction-free space for studying. Keep your phone in another room or turn it off.

3. **Pomodoro Technique:**

- o   Study for 25 minutes, then take a 5-minute break to check your phone. This limits distractions while keeping you refreshed.

Case study:

Sneha was addicted to Instagram and found it hard to concentrate. By using a productivity app and keeping her phone in another room, she regained focus and increased her study hours.

5. Lack of Confidence: Fear of Failure

Challenge:

"The more I study, the more I feel like I'm not good enough."

Story: The Cracked Mirror

A cracked mirror distorts your reflection, making you think you're less than you are. Similarly, self-doubt distorts your view of your abilities.

Techniques:

1. **Positive Affirmations:**

- Start each study session by saying: *"I am improving every day. I am capable of achieving my goals."*

2. **Mistake Notebook:**

   - Instead of fearing mistakes, write them down and learn from them. Over time, this practice turns weaknesses into strengths.

3. **Reach Out:** Talk to a mentor, teacher, or parent when self-doubt creeps in. Often, an external perspective can boost your confidence.

Case study:

Raj felt he wasn't good at Physics. By analyzing mistakes and seeking help from his mentor, he turned his weakest subject into his highest-scoring one in JEE/NEET.

6. Monotony: Losing Interest in the Same Routine

Challenge:

"Studying the same way every day feels boring and unproductive."

Story: The Flat Soda

Even the best soda loses its fizz if left open too long. Similarly, studying the same way every day can drain your enthusiasm.

Techniques:

1. **Change Study Methods:**

   o Alternate between solving questions, watching educational videos, and teaching someone else.

2. **Gamify Your Study:**

   o Set a timer and see how many questions you can solve within 20 minutes.

Compete against yourself to beat your previous score.

3. **Study with Variety:**

   o Study different subjects in blocks (e.g., 2 hours Physics, 1 hour Biology). This keeps your mind engaged.

Case study:

Kavya dreaded her biology sessions. By teaching her sister key concepts, she found a fresh, enjoyable way to study and retain information better.

7. Mental Exhaustion: Feeling Drained and Burnt Out

Challenge:

"I feel tired all the time and can't focus for long periods."

Story: The Empty Tank

You can't drive a car on an empty tank. Similarly, your brain needs regular "refuelling" to stay productive.

Techniques:

1. **Break the Day:**

   o Divide your day into 3–4 focused study blocks with breaks in between. Avoid studying for more than 2 hours at a stretch.

2. **Physical Refreshers:**

   o Take a 10-minute walk, stretch, or do light exercises between study sessions to recharge your mind and body.

3. **Hydration and Nutrition:**

   o Drink plenty of water and eat brain-boosting foods like nuts, fruits, and whole grains to maintain energy levels.

Case study:

In a well-known corporate college, Rohan pushed himself to study 14 hours a day but felt burnt out within a few months. Not able to concentrate, motivated, and gradually decreasing interest even though he is a bright student. By coming out of this non-cooperative environment and switching to a balanced schedule and taking breaks, his productivity and focus improved significantly.

8. Lack of Clarity: Feeling Lost on Where to Start

Challenge:

"I don't know which topics to study or how to organize my time."

Story: The Unmapped Journey

A journey without a map leads to wandering in circles. A clear plan is your map, guiding you to your destination efficiently.

Techniques:

1. **Weekly Planning:**

   - Set weekly goals for subjects and topics. Divide them into smaller daily tasks.

2. **Focus on Priority Topics:**

   - Identify high-weightage topics from past papers and focus on mastering them first.

3. **Checklist Method:**

   - Create a checklist for each subject. Tick off topics as you complete them to visualize progress.

Case study:

Mohan felt lost with his vast JEE/NEET syllabus. By creating a 30-day plan focusing on high-priority topics, he gained clarity and boosted his confidence.

9. The "Plateau Phase" Struggle: Stuck in a Rut

Challenge:

"No matter how much I study my scores seem to stay the same. I feel like I'm not improving."

Story: The Butterfly Struggle

Imagine a caterpillar in a cocoon. From the outside, it looks like nothing is happening. But inside, the caterpillar is transforming into a butterfly. Growth often happens beneath the surface before it becomes visible.

Case study:

One of my students, Arjun, was stuck scoring around 120 in his mock tests. He shifted his approach by focusing on quality over quantity—fewer tests but thorough analysis. In the last 20 days, his scores shot up to 180.

Actionable Insight:

- **Deep Dive Analysis:** After each test, spend twice as much time reviewing mistakes as you did take the test.

- **Micro Improvements:** Identify one weak area daily and improve it. Over time, these small wins compound into big results.

10. Sleep Deprivation: The Silent Saboteur

Challenge:

"I stay up late studying, but I'm always tired and can't focus during the day."

Story: The Charging Phone

Your brain is like a smartphone. Without proper rest, it operates at 10% battery, slowing down and losing efficiency. Sleep isn't a waste of time; it's your body's way of recharging for peak performance.

Quote:

"Sleep is the golden chain that ties health and our bodies together." – Thomas Dekker

Actionable Insight:

- **Sleep Schedule:** Aim for 7–8 hours of sleep daily. Prioritize consistency over duration—going to bed and waking up at the same time.

- **Power Naps:** A 20-minute nap can restore focus during the afternoon slump.

- **Wind-Down Ritual:** Avoid screens for 30 minutes before bed. Instead, read something light or practice relaxation techniques.

11. Comparing with Others: The Confidence Killer

Challenge:

"My friends are scoring higher than me. Will I ever catch up?"

Story: The Racehorse Blinkers

Racehorses wear blinkers to block distractions and focus solely on their lane. Comparing yourself to others is like running a race while constantly looking sideways—it slows you down.

Case study:

Meera, a NEET aspirant, spent months comparing her scores to her classmates'. Once she stopped and focused solely on improving her weaknesses, she outperformed most of them in the final exam.

Quote:

"Don't compare your Chapter 1 to someone else's Chapter 20."

Actionable Insight:

- **Progress Journal:** Document your daily improvements, no matter how small. Use these as proof of your growth.

- **Social Media Detox:** Avoid platforms where others post about their preparation. Focus on your journey.

12. Family Expectations: The Invisible Weight

Challenge:

"My family expects so much from me. I'm scared of disappointing them."

Story: The Kite and the Wind

A kite needs wind to fly, but too much wind can cause it to crash. Family expectations can be motivating, but they must be balanced to avoid becoming overwhelming.

Case study:

Priya, a NEET student, had constant pressure from her parents. Instead of bottling it up, she had an open conversation with them, setting realistic expectations. This reduced her stress and boosted her performance.

Actionable Insight:

Communicate: Share your progress and challenges with your family. Involve them in celebrating small wins.

- **Set Boundaries:** Politely ask for uninterrupted study hours.

The Seedling in the Storm

A seedling faces storms, rain, and harsh winds, but it keeps growing. Your preparation journey may feel hard now, but every challenge is helping you grow stronger.

Quote:

"Hard times create strong people. The struggle you're facing today is building the strength you need for tomorrow."

Summary:

"When things feel hard, remind yourself that progress isn't always visible immediately. Every small effort you make today is paving the way for your success tomorrow. Keep moving forward."

Next chapter dealt with a detailed framework addressing the **struggles of constant comparison with others** and the **perceived partiality from teachers and parents**, along with actionable strategies, and motivational stories to guide students toward self-confidence and focus.

CHAPTER 2

Overcoming Comparison and Bias

In the competitive environment of JEE/NEET preparation, it is easy to become locked in a loop of comparison. The frequent comparison of grades, accomplishments, and growth with classmates might cause you to question your worth, leaving you feeling inadequate and demoralised. At the same time, apparent favouritism, whether from instructors or parents, can exacerbate the emotional strain by making you feel overlooked or unfairly assessed. These problems, albeit frequently unsaid, weigh hard on many aspirants, preventing them from focusing on their individual skills and ambitions. Even such problems bothered **the great warrior of all time Arjuna,** let's understand Arjuna's story from the epic Mahabharata.

Mahabharata: Arjuna's Struggle with Comparison

In the **Mahabharata**, Arjuna's journey as a warrior was not without moments of self-doubt and the heavy burden of comparison. Despite being Dronacharya's favourite student, Arjuna often felt overshadowed by the extraordinary skills of Karna and Ekalavya.

Karna, with his natural talent and fearless spirit, seemed almost invincible. Ekalavya, despite being denied formal training, became a master archer on his own, surpassing many in skill and precision. Witnessing their abilities, Arjuna began to question himself:

"Am I truly the best? What if I'm destined to always be second to someone else?"

This comparison started clouding his mind, weakening his confidence. Arjuna felt restless, unable to focus on his practice. Sensing his turmoil, Krishna—his guide and mentor—stepped in.

Krishna's Powerful Lesson on Self-Worth

Krishna took Arjuna to a quiet riverbank and said, **"Arjuna, what do you see when you look at the river?"** Arjuna replied, **"I see the water flowing peacefully."** Krishna smiled and asked, **"What if the river compared itself to the ocean or a small stream? Would it change its nature?"**

Arjuna thought for a moment. Krishna continued, **"Every being has its own unique path. You are not Karna, nor are you, Ekalavya. Their journeys are theirs alone. If you waste your energy on comparison, you will stray from your purpose. Focus on your practice, trust your journey, and greatness will follow."**

How Arjuna Overcame Comparison

From that day forward, Arjuna redirected his energy inward. He stopped worrying about how others performed and concentrated solely on perfecting his own skills. He practiced harder than ever, mastering techniques that no other archer could match.

Most importantly, **he embraced his individuality**, realizing that his destiny was unique, and no one else's success could diminish his own potential.

By overcoming the trap of comparison, Arjuna became a warrior unparalleled in skill and focus. His story reminds us that success is not about being better than others, it's about becoming the best version of yourself.

In the same way, this chapter serves as a roadmap for breaking free from these mental constraints. It provides practical answers to aid you.

Move Beyond Comparison: Change your attention from outward validation to internal advancement, focusing on personal growth rather than comparing oneself to others.

Handle perceived favouritism: Learn how to confront feelings of bias constructively, whether from professors or parents, while keeping your self-esteem and motivation.

Improve Self-Worth: Create confidence that is not

dependent on other people's opinions or behaviours, allowing you to shine regardless of the circumstances.

Turn Negativity into Drive: Turn sentiments of being neglected into motivation for self-improvement, demonstrating via actions that your efforts are worthy of praise.

This chapter will help you realise that your journey is unique to you by providing relatable anecdotes, useful solutions, and motivating metaphors. Comparisons and perceived prejudices can distract you, but they do not define you.

Remember that success isn't about being noticed; it's about living up to your potential and achieving your goals on your own terms. This chapter will teach you how to rise above the noise, embrace your uniqueness, and convert every obstacle into an opportunity for progress. You only need focus, resilience, and self-belief to achieve, regardless of the distractions surrounding you.

1. Constant Comparison with Others

Challenge:

"I keep comparing my progress and scores with my peers, and it makes me feel like I'm not good enough."

Story: The Garden of Growth

Imagine a garden with different plants—some are roses, others are sunflowers, and some are tall trees. Each grows at its own pace and in its own way. A rose doesn't compare itself to a tree because they're both beautiful in their uniqueness. Similarly, *when each plant receives the right support—adequate light, water, and minerals—it flourishes into the best, most unmatchable version of itself, showcasing its unique qualities to the fullest.*

Actionable Techniques:

1. **Track Your Own Progress:**
   - Maintain a personal "Progress Journal." Compare where you were last week with where you are today, not with others.
   - Focus on the improvement in your mock test scores or the number of topics you've mastered.

2. **Set Individual Benchmarks:**
   - Shift your mindset from *"I need to beat them"* to *"I need to beat yesterday's me."*
   - Replace phrases like *"They're better than me"* with *"I'm getting better each day."*

3. **Limit Peer Discussions:**

- o Avoid unnecessary discussions about test scores or preparation strategies with friends if they cause you stress.

Story:

Sneha often compared her test scores with her friend, Ramesh, who consistently scored higher. She realized that focusing on her weaknesses rather than his strengths was the key to improvement. By tracking her progress, she improved her Physics scores by 30% in a month.

Quote:

"You can't compare the moon's glow to the sun's brilliance, yet both light up the world in their own time."

2. The Role of Social Media in Comparison

Challenge:

"Seeing others post about their preparation or achievements makes me feel left behind."

Story: The Mirage in the Desert

Social media often shows only the highlights of someone's life, like a mirage in the desert. It's not the full picture and can lead you astray.

Actionable Techniques:

1. **Social Media Detox:**

   - Deactivate or limit your time on platforms during your preparation period. Use apps like StayFocusd to block distracting sites.

2. **Filter Content:**

   - Follow accounts that provide motivation, study tips, or positivity. Unfollow those that stress you out.

3. **Reframe Social Media Posts:**

   - Instead of feeling envious, think: *"If they can achieve this, so can I."*

3. Teachers Showing Partiality

Challenge:

"I feel like my teachers favour other students and don't pay enough attention to me."

Story: The Shadow in the Spotlight

In a theatre, the spotlight focuses on one actor, but that doesn't mean the others aren't important to the play. Similarly, even if a teacher seems to favour someone, your value as a student remains significant.

Actionable Techniques:

1. **Seek Constructive Feedback:**

   o Politely ask the teacher for specific feedback on your performance. For example: *"I'd like to improve in this topic—can you suggest how I should approach it?"*

   o This shows initiative and encourages them to focus on your growth.

2. **Be Your Own Guide:**

   o Remember that self-study is the most critical component of success. Don't let perceived favouritism affect your efforts.

3. **Leverage Other Resources:**

   o Use online platforms, peers, or other mentors to fill in any gaps if you feel a teacher isn't supporting you enough.

Story:

Priya believed her Chemistry teacher favoured a top-performing student. Instead of feeling left out, she used it as a challenge and followed consistently study guides, allowing her to know her mistake and correct immediately and not allowing them to repeat, with patience she became master the subject, ultimately scoring higher than her classmate.

Quote:

"Life isn't about waiting for someone to notice you, it's about making yourself impossible to ignore."

4. Dealing with Emotional Impact

Challenge:

"I feel demotivated and upset when I'm overlooked or compared by teachers."

Story: The Eagle and the Sparrow

An eagle soars high above the ground, unaffected by the chatter of sparrows. Similarly, focusing on your own goals will help you rise above petty comparisons or favouritism.

Actionable Techniques:

1. **Reframe Teacher Comments:**

   - If a teacher compares you to another student, use it as motivation: *"What can I learn from them to improve myself?"*

   - Avoid taking comments personally. Remember, teachers may unintentionally favour students, but it doesn't diminish your potential.

2. **Channel Emotions Productively:**

   - Pour your frustration into focused study sessions. Treat every moment of hard work as proof of your determination.

3. **Talk to a Mentor or Parent:**

   - Share your feelings with someone you trust. Sometimes, a different perspective can help you see the situation more objectively.

Quote:

"Your value doesn't decrease based on someone's inability to see your worth."

5. Building Self-Worth

Challenge:

"How do I stop seeking validation from teachers or peers?"

Story: The Banyan Tree of the Village

In a small village, a majestic banyan tree stands at the center. It provides shade, shelter, and a meeting place for all, yet it doesn't grow to seek anyone's approval. Its strength comes from its deep roots and spreading branches, nurtured by the soil and sun.

Like the banyan tree, your self-worth should come from your inner roots—your values, culture, and strengths—not from the praise or opinions of others. Stand firm in who you are, and let your actions speak for themselves, becoming a source of inspiration and comfort to those around you.

Actionable Techniques:

1. **Self-Affirmations:**

    - Repeat daily: *"I am capable, hardworking, and improving every day. My efforts define me, not someone else's opinion."*

2. **Focus on Mastery, Not Approval:**

   o   Set personal goals and celebrate achieving them. For instance, if you solve a tough question, acknowledge it as your victory, regardless of external validation.

3. **Gratitude Practice:**

   o   At the end of the day, write down three things you're proud of about yourself. This shifts your focus from seeking approval to self-appreciation.

Story:

Meena used to feel invisible in her class. By shifting her focus to personal achievements, she gained confidence and realized that success doesn't depend on others noticing you.

Quote:

"Confidence is not in being flawless, but in embracing your imperfections and learning from them." – R.K. Narayan

The Sculptor and the Marble

A sculptor doesn't wait for applause during the process of carving a statue. They keep chiselling away, knowing the masterpiece will emerge in time. You are both the sculptor and the masterpiece—focus on refining yourself, and recognition will follow naturally.

Take away:

Comparison and favouritism may seem like obstacles, but they're distractions. Focus on your growth, trust your efforts, and let your results speak louder than anything else.

CHAPTER 3

From Frustration to Mastery - Overcoming Dislike of a Subject

IN your JEE/NEET preparation, there will always be parts of the syllabus that excite you—topics you enjoy solving or concepts that come naturally. But then there are the ones that feel tedious or overwhelming, like a mountain of tasks you'd rather avoid, or some students have at least one subject that they dread because it feels unattainable or dull. Everything's easy to put everything aside and concentrate on the ones you appreciate. However, avoiding a subject does not make it disappear; instead, it exacerbates the problem. Over time, this hatred can lead to worry, procrastination, and even a fear of failure.

Dislike of a subject has far-reaching consequences:

It causes gaps in your preparation, rendering specific elements of your curriculum ineffective and untrustworthy.

- It saps your energy and concentration as you struggle with the mental resistance to studying it.
- It sows seeds of self-doubt, prompting you to question your overall ability.

The truth is that, with the correct attitude and method, any subject—no matter how difficult it may appear now—can be mastered. You will learn how to change the way you feel about your least favourite subject in this chapter.

"Ever wonder why some people push through challenges while others give up? The answer lies in mastering frustration and turning setbacks into steppingstones for lifelong success."

Let's understand more about the frustration in one's success or failure.

The Frustration Barrier: The First Step to Mastery

Overcoming frustration is not just a skill—it's a powerful predictor of success in academics and life. Those who develop **high frustration tolerance** are more likely to exhibit qualities such as **self-control, courage, and resilience,** all of which are critical for **high performance and academic excellence.**

But what exactly is this **Frustration Barrier**?

It's that **initial phase** of skill acquisition where everything feels slow, difficult, and far from enjoyable. **Progress seems invisible,** and it's tempting to quit. For many, this is where they stop, convinced they lack the necessary talent. But the **true masters of learning** push through this barrier, turning frustration into fuel.

Research from Anders Ericsson highlights that those who thrive in this phase have learned the **meta-skill of overcoming frustration**, making it easier to learn and master any discipline. In fact, **a study on Chinese college teachers** showed a strong link between **frustration tolerance and academic performance**, proving that how you handle setbacks is just as important as raw ability.

The Power of Self-Compassion: Your Secret Weapon to overcome frustration

While grit and discipline are important, there's another hidden element that helps top performers stay on course during tough times: **Self-Compassion.**

According to **Dr. Kristin Neff**, self-compassion is the practice of being kind to yourself in moments of failure or difficulty. **It's not about making excuses—it's about staying balanced and positive even when things go wrong.**

- Studies show that **self-compassion reduces anxiety and burnout** while improving **resilience and performance.**

- Elite athletes like **Novak Djokovic** rely on self-compassion to bounce back from setbacks, avoiding the destructive spiral of self-criticism.

Strategies for Breaking Through the Frustration Barrier

1. **Admit Your Limitations**

   Let go of your ego and acknowledge that you're not perfect. This humility makes it easier to focus on learning and improvement, rather than protecting your self-image.

2. **Surround Yourself with the Right People**

   Want to learn faster? Immerse yourself in communities of **high performers**. Seeing others who've overcome similar challenges reinforces the belief that mastery is possible.

3. **Study the Masters**

   Research how top performers in your field succeeded. This will expose you to practical ideas for improvement and strengthen your confidence in the process of skill-building.

4. **Find Joy in the Challenge**

    Shift your mindset from frustration to excitement. Think of each obstacle as a puzzle that sharpens your mind and resilience.

5. **Commit to Consistent Practice**

    There's no substitute for regular, disciplined effort. When internal resistance kicks in, remind yourself that consistency is the key to building momentum and eventually crossing the barrier.

    Remember **"Frustration is Temporary, Growth is Permanent"**

The following simple yet powerful Zen story will help shift your thought process about disliking something.

ZEN MASTER STORY:

A young monk once approached his Zen master, frustrated with the daily chores of the monastery—**carrying water from the river, chopping firewood, and sweeping the floors**. He believed these tasks were menial, far removed from the higher purpose of spiritual enlightenment. **He felt trapped by the repetitive routine,** thinking, *"How can I reach enlightenment when my time is wasted on such trivial things?"*

One day, unable to contain his frustration, he approached the master and asked, **"Why must I waste time doing things I dislike? Aren't they distractions from my true path?"**

The Zen master smiled calmly and replied, **"Before enlightenment, we carry water and chop wood. After enlightenment, we carry water and chop wood."**

Confused, the monk stared at the master, waiting for an explanation. **"What does that mean?"** he asked.

The master patiently explained,

"Carrying water and chopping wood are not distractions; they are the practice itself. Everything—whether you like it or not—contributes to your growth. The key is to be fully present in whatever you do. Even the tasks you dislike can teach you something essential. If you avoid them, you miss an opportunity for growth."

The monk was still unsure but promised to reflect on the master's words. Over the next few weeks, he tried a new approach. Instead of rushing through his chores with resentment, **he began paying close attention to every detail.** He felt the weight of the water buckets on his shoulders, heard the rhythmic sound of the axe cutting through the wood, and noticed how sweeping cleared not just the floor but also his thoughts.

Gradually, **his frustration transformed into clarity**. He realized that the chores were not a distraction at all—they were training his mind and body. Carrying water strengthened his endurance. Chopping wood taught him focus and precision. Sweeping the floor brought a sense of calm and order to his thoughts. These daily tasks, which he once resisted, became an integral part of his spiritual journey.

He learned that **growth is not always found in grand, extraordinary moments. It is built slowly, in the seemingly small and repetitive actions of daily life.** We need to understand that when the monk reflected on this and began approaching his chores with a new mindset, gradually, he realized that those very tasks he disliked helped him build patience, strength, and discipline—qualities essential for his spiritual journey.The chores taught him patience, discipline, and the ability to stay present—exactly what he needed for enlightenment. But in your JEE/NEET preparation, every subject is equally important and offers an opportunity to improve your skills. Now, let's move on to your scenarios.

1. Disliking a Subject: Turning Weakness into Strength

Challenge:

"I can't stand this subject! It feels boring, difficult, or irrelevant to my success."

Story: The Unpolished Gem

Imagine a rough, dull stone that looks uninteresting at first glance. But with consistent effort and polishing, it transforms into a brilliant gem. That disliked subject might be your rough stone now but mastering it could become one of your brightest achievements.

Techniques to Overcome Subject Hatred:

1. **Understand the Importance:**
   - Research how this subject contributes to your exam success and overall goal.

- o For instance, Physics might be tough but mastering it could boost your rank significantly due to its weightage.

2. **Start Small:**

   - o Begin with the simplest topics. Gaining confidence in small areas creates a foundation for tackling harder concepts.

3. **Use Different Resources:**

   - o If your textbook or teacher's style doesn't click with you, try YouTube videos, podcasts, or alternative guides. Sometimes a fresh perspective makes all the difference.

4. **Gamify Learning:**

   - o Turn the subject into a challenge. E.g., reward yourself for solving 10 questions or completing a topic.

Case study:

Ravi hated Chemistry, especially Organic Reactions. By

starting with reaction mechanisms (which seemed easier), using visual aids like reaction maps, and practicing one reaction daily, he slowly grew to understand and even appreciate the subject.

Quote:

"The expert in anything was once a beginner." – Helen Hayes

2. Strategies to Boost Energy for a Disliked Subject

Challenge:

"Even when I try, I feel drained and lack the energy to focus on this subject."

Story: The Potter and the Wheel

In a small village, there was a skilled potter who created beautiful pots on his wheel. At first, the clay was rough and hard to shape, but with careful, patient effort, the potter would gradually mold it into something fine. The wheel would spin slowly at first, but with each turn, the clay became smoother and more malleable.

In today's world, when faced with a subject you dislike, it's like working with a difficult piece of clay. The initial effort may feel slow, and progress might seem hard to see, but just like the potter's wheel, small, consistent steps will eventually help shape mastery. With regular focus and breaks, just like recharging a device, your energy will renew, and you'll find yourself making steady progress in even the toughest subjects.

Techniques to Recharge Energy:

1. **Set Time Limits:**

   o Study the disliked subject in short bursts (e.g., 25 minutes) instead of long sessions to avoid burning out.

2. **Pair It with a Favourite Subject:**

o Follow up a session of the disliked subject with one you enjoy. This creates a mental reward loop.

3. **Visualize Success:**

   o Imagine how confident you'll feel when you finally master the subject and see improvement in your mock test scores.

4. **Celebrate Progress:**

   o Even completing a small chapter or solving a few problems deserves a pat on the back.

Case study:

Neha dreaded Biology but knew it was crucial for NEET. She created colorful mind maps and quizzed herself after every topic. Slowly, her energy and interest grew, and she began scoring consistently well.

Quote:

"Strength doesn't come from what you can do. It comes from overcoming the things you once thought you couldn't." – Rikki Rogers

3. Preoccupied Thoughts: Clearing Mental Clutter

Challenge:

"My mind keeps wandering, thinking about everything except my studies."

Story: The Cloudy Sky

Preoccupied thoughts are like clouds blocking the sun—they prevent clarity and focus. But just as clouds drift away, you can clear your mind and let your energy shine through.

Techniques to Clear Mental Clutter:

- **Mind Dumping:**

- Write down everything that's bothering you on paper. This releases your mind from holding onto those thoughts.

2. **5-Minute Reset:**
   - Pause, close your eyes, and take deep breaths. Focus on the sensation of breathing to ground yourself in the present moment.

3. **Practice Time Blocking:**
   - Dedicate specific times to worrying or daydreaming. E.g., *"I'll think about this issue for 10 minutes at 7 PM."* This helps you stay present during study hours.

4. **Anchor Yourself with a Question:**
   - When distracted, ask yourself: *"Is this thought helping me achieve my goal?"* If not, gently return your focus to the task at hand.

Case study:

Amit found himself constantly worrying about his performance. By journaling his thoughts every morning and practicing short meditation sessions, he improved his concentration and reduced mental distractions.

Quote:

"You can't stop the waves, but you can learn to surf." – Jon Kabat-Zinn

4. Transforming Preoccupied Thoughts into Productivity

Challenge:

"I feel stuck in negative thoughts and don't know how to refocus."

Story: The Broken Compass

Preoccupied thoughts act like a broken compass, spinning aimlessly and making you lose direction. Fixing the compass (your focus) points you back toward your goals.

Techniques to Redirect Energy:

1. **Break the Thought Cycle:**

    - Stand up, stretch, or take a brisk walk to interrupt negative thought patterns.

Physical movement resets your mental state.

2. **Reframe the Thought:**

   o Instead of thinking *"I'll never finish this chapter,"* reframe it to *"I'll finish just the first section for now."*

3. **Visualization Technique:**

   o Picture a "thought container" in your mind. Imagine placing your worries inside it, sealing it, and putting it aside for later.

4. **Positive Substitution:**

   o Replace thoughts like *"I can't do this"* with *"I've overcome tough challenges before, and I'll do it again."*

Case study:

Megha's mind wandered constantly during self-study, thinking about exams and peer pressure. By using the "thought container" technique and practicing gratitude, she reclaimed her focus and energy.

Quote:

"You are the master of your mind, not its servant." –
Robin Sharma

5. Creating a Positive Environment

Challenge:

"I don't feel motivated or energized to study in my current setup."

Story: The Lotus in the Muddy Pond

A lotus blooms beautifully, but it thrives in the murky waters of a pond. Though surrounded by mud, it rises above and flourishes with the right balance of sunlight and nourishment. Similarly, focus and energy are essential to success, no matter how difficult the surroundings may be. Just as the lotus rises from the mud, you too can rise above distractions and obstacles. Success is not defined by luxurious surroundings or high status—it's the ability to maintain focus and energy in any environment that determines true achievement. At later stages, however, taking advantage of better external conditions—like strong support systems or advanced resources—can amplify your growth, but it is your internal strength and persistence that lays the foundation for success.

Techniques to Improve the Environment:

1. **Organize Your Space:**

   - Keep your study area clean and clutter-free. A tidy space promotes a tidy mind.

2. **Incorporate Positivity:**

- Place motivational quotes, pictures of your goal college, or a vision board near your study desk.

3. **Use Natural Light:**

   - Study in a well-lit area to boost alertness.

4. **Ambient Soundscapes:**

   - Use calming music or white noise to create a focused atmosphere.

Case study:

Karthik felt demotivated studying in his messy room. By decluttering his desk and adding a vision board with his dream college, he created a more positive environment and improved his productivity.

Quote:

"Your environment shapes your productivity." – James Clear

The Phoenix Rising from Ashes

When you hate a subject or feel drained by preoccupied thoughts, remind yourself of the phoenix. It rises from its ashes, stronger and more radiant than before. You, too, have the power to rise above challenges, find your energy, and turn weaknesses into strengths.

TAKE AWAY:

"The things you find hardest now are your greatest opportunities for growth. With the right mindset, every disliked subject and distracting thought can become steppingstones to your success."

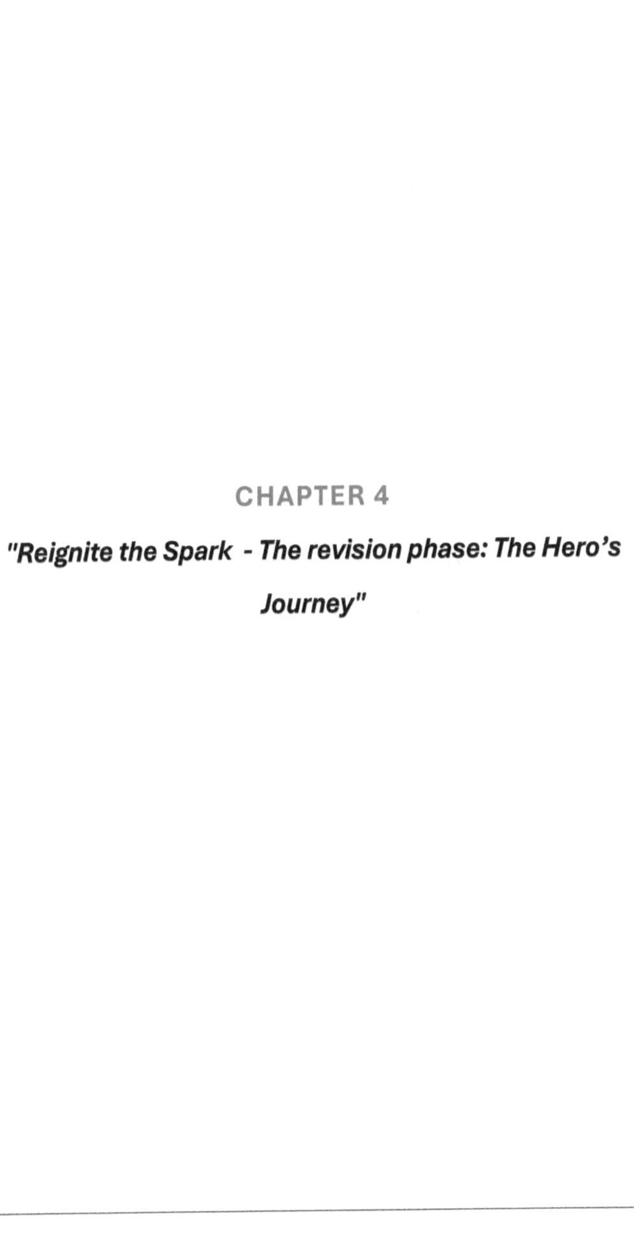

CHAPTER 4

"Reignite the Spark - The revision phase: The Hero's

Journey"

*"**E** very hero faces challenges that test their limits. Preparing for JEE/NEET/NEET is your hero's journey, filled with ups, downs, victories, and lessons. The final leg of this journey—the revision phase—is where champions are made. Let's arm you with strategies to overcome every obstacle in your way!"*

A prevalent and intimidating obstacle that many students confront as the last days of JEE/NEET preparation draw near is the anxiety of revision. The idea of going over a lot of material again can make you feel overwhelmed rather than confident and prepared to consolidate all you've learnt. The strain increases with each day that goes by, and the clock is ticking. Will I recall everything? Will the pressure in the exam room be too much for me to handle? These thoughts race through your head, frequently making you feel more anxious rather than more capable of succeeding.

However, what if editing didn't have to seem like a time crunch? What if you were able to approach it with confidence, clarity, and control? Revision doesn't have to be a scary thing; it can be the last piece of information that turns all of your knowledge into mastery and unlocks your potential.

This chapter will teach you how to organize, plan, and carry out your revision with purpose and accuracy so that you are not overwhelmed by the sheer volume of content that still has to be covered. You can change revision from a cause of anxiety to a last boost of confidence before the big day by tackling your last preparations with composure and organization.

Keep in mind that the final step of preparation is about mastering what you have already learnt and having faith in your ability to perform at your best, not about cramming or racing against the clock. Together, we can make this last phase of your journey the most impactful one yet. Let's try to understand how the world class players make themselves super powerful with their strategies.

What's the Secret Behind the Success of Top Performers?

Have you ever wondered how athletes like **Michael Phelps, Serena Williams, and LeBron James** consistently stay at the top? What's their secret? It's not just talent or luck—it's their unmatched ability to prepare, practice, and improve continuously. The same principles can be applied to students preparing for competitive exams like JEE, NEET, or board exams. Success lies in adopting these strategies and building habits like the world's top performers. Curious how they do it? Let's break it down into three key areas:

1. Mental Preparation and Mindset

Mental toughness is the backbone of every top performer. Athletes prepare their minds as much as their bodies. This mental preparation helps them stay calm under pressure, overcome nerves, and focus on their goals. Here's how **elite performers** do it:

- **Michael Phelps – Visualization Master**
  Before every race, Michael Phelps mentally rehearses his entire swim—from start to finish. He visualizes every stroke, every breath, and even possible challenges. When the actual race happens, it feels familiar and manageable.

How to Apply It: Visualize yourself sitting in the exam hall, confidently answering questions. Practice this every day to build calmness and control over your nerves.

- **LeBron James – Mental Rehearsal and Mindfulness**

LeBron mentally plays out different game scenarios before stepping onto the court. He also practices mindfulness to stay present and focused.

How to Apply It: During your revision, mentally rehearse tough questions and visualize success. Use deep breathing to stay focused when anxiety strikes.

2. Efficient Study and Revision Methods

Top performers in both sports and academics follow a planned, focused approach to training and study. They use active learning and specific strategies to make the most of their practice sessions.

- **Serena Williams – The Power of Micro-Goals**
  Serena focuses on improving one small thing at a time during practice, knowing that these small improvements will add up to big wins.

How to Apply It: Focus on one weak topic each day. Break it down into small, achievable goals, and track your progress.

- **Novak Djokovic – Periodization and Strategic Planning**

  Djokovic divides his training into specific periods, with each phase focusing on a particular goal—skills, endurance, or recovery.

How to Apply It: Plan your study schedule in phases. Start with concept building, move to practice, and leave time for full-length mock tests before the exam.

---

3. Continuous Improvement and Habit Formation

The world's best performers never settle. They constantly reflect, refine, and improve their methods, turning feedback and failures into fuel for growth.

- **Roger Federer – Reflection and Self-Analysis**

  Federer regularly reflects on his performance to identify areas for improvement. He doesn't just focus on winning but on refining every aspect of his game.

How to Apply It: After every mock test, analyze your mistakes and learn from them. Develop strategies to avoid repeating those mistakes.

- **Stephen Curry – The Power of Feedback**
  Curry constantly seeks feedback from coaches to improve his game. He's open to criticism and uses it as a tool for growth.

How to Apply It: Seek feedback from your teachers or peers. Be open to constructive criticism and use it to get better.

The Secret Lies in Your Hands: Start Building Your Winning Routine

These top performers didn't become legends overnight. Their success came from **small, consistent efforts**, combined with smart strategies and continuous improvement.

You have the power to do the same! Whether it's practicing visualization like Michael Phelps, setting micro-goals like Serena Williams, or reflecting on your performance like Roger Federer, **every small habit you build today will lead you to long-term success**.

Now, let's understand our daily routine in our exact contest.

1. Understanding Revision Challenges

Challenge 1: Procrastination

- *"I'll start after this..."* Sound familiar? Procrastination steals valuable time, but it can be defeated.

Techniques:

1. **Pomodoro Technique**: Work for 25 minutes, take a 5-minute break, and repeat. Use an app like Forest to stay disciplined.

2. **2-Minute Rule**: Commit to starting a task for just two minutes. Often, starting is the hardest part.

3. **Visual Countdown**: Create a large calendar with days left for the exam. Physically crossing off days builds urgency.

Challenge 2: Difficulty Prioritizing Topics

- *"Where do I even begin? There's so much to cover!"*

Techniques:

1. **ABC Analysis:**

- o   A: High-weightage topics (Physics: Mechanics, Chemistry: Organic, Biology: Genetics)

- o   B: Medium-weightage topics

- o   C: Lesser-weightage topics
  Revise A daily, B every other day, and glance through C in spare time.

2. **80/20 Rule**: Focus 80% of your energy on 20% of topics that carry maximum marks.

3. **Visual Aids**: Use sticky notes to list top topics on your study table.

Challenge 3: Low Confidence After Mock Tests

- *"I'm scoring so low. Am I even cut out for this?"*

Techniques:

1. **Mistake Notebook:**

   - o   Dedicate a notebook to write down all mistakes and their solutions. Review it daily—it's a goldmine of improvement areas.

2. **Success Journal**: Write one thing you got right after every test. Celebrate small wins to stay motivated.

3. **3-Step Reflection Process**:
   - **Step 1:** What went wrong?
   - **Step 2:** Why did it go wrong?
   - **Step 3:** How can I avoid it next time?

Challenge 4: Lack of Focus

- *"I can't sit for long hours without getting distracted."*

Techniques:

1. **Digital Detox**:
   - Install apps like StayFocusd to block social media during study hours.
   - Keep your phone in another room while studying.

2. **Deep Work Blocks**: Schedule 90-minute focused sessions followed by a 20-minute break.

3. **Anchoring**: Begin every session with a short ritual—e.g., lighting a candle or playing calming music—to signal your brain it's time to focus.

Challenge 5: Fear of Failure

- *"What if I don't make it? I'll let everyone down."*

Techniques:

1. **Positive Visualization**: Every morning, close your eyes and imagine yourself achieving your dream rank.

2. **Mantra for Resilience**: Repeat this daily: *"I am stronger than my fears. Every mistake is a step toward success."*

3. **Perspective Shift**: Write down the worst-case scenario, then list ways to bounce back from it. Often, the fear reduces when you confront it logically.

2. Crafting a Solid Revision Plan

Daily Structure:(*Just suggestable but need to tailor it for your needs*)

1. **Morning**: Revise core concepts and weak topics (3 hours).

2. **Afternoon**: Solve 50 topic-specific questions (2 hours).

3. **Evening**: Take one mock test (3 hours).

4. **Night**: Analyze mistakes and revise formulas (2 hours).

Weekly Strategy:

- **3+1 Revision Cycle:**

    o   3 days: Intense revision of different subjects.

    o   1 day: Full-length test and analysis.

3. Building Emotional Resilience

Challenge: Burnout During Revision

- *"I'm so tired; I feel like giving up."*

Techniques:

1. **Recharge Routine:**

    o   After every 90-minute session, take a walk, stretch, or listen to a motivational podcast.

- o   It includes at least 30 minutes of physical activity daily.

2. **Power Naps**: A 20-minute nap can refresh your mind for another productive session.

3. **Gratitude Practice**: Write down three things you're grateful for each night. This keeps your morale high.

4. Mastering Self-Discipline

Challenge: Irregular Study Hours

- *"Some days I study a lot; other days I slack off."*

Techniques:

1. **Same Time, Same Place**: Study at the same time and location daily to create a habit loop.

2. **Accountability Partner**: Pair up with a friend to track each other's daily goals.

3. **Reward System**: Treat yourself (e.g., a movie night or favorite snack) after completing weekly goals.

5. Harnessing Resources

Challenge: Feeling Overwhelmed by Material

- *"There's too much material. I don't know what to focus on."*

Techniques:

1. **Resource Audit**: Stick to two trusted books per subject and limit extra reference material.

2. **One-Page Summaries**: Create summary sheets for formulas, reactions, and concepts.

3. **Selective Practice**: Solve only previous years' questions for certain chapters.

---

6. Strengthening Mental Endurance

Challenge: Giving Up Midway

- *"I don't think I can handle this anymore."*

Techniques:

1. **Micro-Goals**: Focus on completing the next chapter or solving 10 questions instead of the entire syllabus.

2. **Break the Pattern**: When overwhelmed, switch to an enjoyable topic or take a 10-minute

motivational break (watch inspiring success stories).

3. **Support Network**: Share your struggles with mentors, parents, or friends who can lift you up.

7. Celebrating Progress

Challenge: Feeling Like No Progress Is Happening

- *"I've been studying so much, but I still feel stuck."*

Techniques:

1. **Progress Tracker**: Maintain a checklist and tick off topics as you revise them. Seeing tangible progress boosts confidence.

2. **Weekly Reflection**: Spend 10 minutes every Sunday to review what you've achieved and plan the week ahead.

3. **Reward Yourself**: Celebrate milestones—e.g., finishing the syllabus, improving mock test scores.

"Inspiration Capsule"

The Story of Usain Bolt: How Preparation and Precision Led to Glory

Usain Bolt's incredible speed and charisma earned him the title of the fastest man alive. But his success didn't happen overnight—it was the result of years of meticulous preparation, self-correction, and relentless focus on accuracy.

1. Identifying and Correcting Weaknesses

Early in his career, Bolt's biggest weakness was his **starting block technique**. His tall frame made it harder for him to accelerate in the first few meters, often putting him behind competitors at the start. Bolt and his coach didn't ignore this weakness. **They focused on breaking the race into smaller parts** and improving the first 30 meters of his sprint.

- **Practical Strategy**: Bolt practiced his starts repeatedly, analysing videos of every run to see where he was losing milliseconds. He made slight adjustments in his body position, reaction time, and pushing technique to improve his take-off speed.
- **Result**: His split time for the first 30 meters

improved significantly, allowing him to dominate the race right from the start.

2. Building Mental Toughness and Focus

Training for years with the pressure to perform at the Olympics is mentally exhausting. Bolt experienced several setbacks, including injuries and losses in practice races. He admitted that staying motivated and mentally sharp was often harder than physical training. **To overcome this, Bolt worked on his mental game as much as his physical one.**

- **Practical Strategy**: Bolt used **visualization techniques**, mentally rehearsing every detail of the race—how he would react to the starting gun, how his body would move at each phase, and how he would finish strong. He also built a routine of listening to music to stay relaxed and focused before every race.

- **Result**: When race day came, Bolt felt calm and confident. He had already "run the race" in his mind countless times. This mental preparation gave him a significant edge over competitors who were tense or distracted by pressure.

3. Perfecting the Smallest Details

While most athletes focus on speed and power, Bolt paid close attention to even the smallest elements of his race. He worked on improving his **stride length, breathing patterns, and foot placement** to maximize efficiency. He and his coach treated each training session like a laboratory experiment—constantly testing and refining every detail.

- **Practical Strategy**: Bolt didn't just rely on hard work. **He embraced data and technology**, using video analysis and biomechanical feedback to make small improvements that added up to major gains.
- **Result**: By perfecting the details, Bolt gained milliseconds on every part of the race, turning good performances into world records.

Conclusion: The Final Push

- *"You've come this far, and quitting now is not an option. Remember, the real challenge isn't the exam but staying consistent and believing in yourself. These 50 days are a golden opportunity to secure your dream—make every second count."*

- **Mantra:** *"Success is not about luck; it's about preparation, resilience, and relentless effort. I can and will do this."*

CHAPTER 5

The Strength of Minor Victories - How Every Day Contributes to Your Achievement

E ach JEE/NEET preparation day is like a single brick in your success's foundation. On certain days, you'll feel invincible, your concentration steady, you're thinking keen. On other days, it will seem like the objective is unachievable and every step is a battle. However, you could be unaware that every little thing you do, every obstacle you overcome, and every moment of perseverance adds to your larger journey. Success isn't necessarily defined by major discoveries; sometimes, it's the ability to create momentum and change your course through little victories.

When a teacher, parent, or motivator encourages you with powerful words, it feels great, right? It might even push you to study harder or perform better for a few days. But how long does that motivation last? A day? A week? Maybe just until the next challenge knocks you down?

Here's the real question:

What keeps you motivated for the long haul? Is it another inspiring speech? A motivational video? Or waiting for someone else to push you forward?

Do you know what truly makes the difference in long-term motivation?

It's not external praise or big accomplishments. **It's hidden within you—your own small victories.** Yes, those tiny moments of progress that most people overlook are the secret to building unstoppable confidence and sustained motivation.

According to **Teresa Amabile and Steven Kramer's research** (*The Progress Principle*), **minor wins**—like mastering a tough concept, completing a practice test, or sticking to a study schedule—activate the brain's reward system. This release of dopamine builds momentum, making you feel good about your progress and hungry for more success. Their study published in the *Harvard Business Review* found that **small wins are more powerful than major breakthroughs for long-term engagement and motivation**.

So, stop waiting for someone to motivate you. **Your power lies in recognizing your small wins.** Celebrate them, track them, and watch how they transform your mindset.

We'll take inspiration from inspirational tales that emphasis the value of perseverance, consistency, and little triumphs in this chapter. These tales will serve as a reminder that your achievement is shaped by every study session, concentrated hour, and perseverance-testing endeavour.

1. The Compass Metaphor: Find Your True North

Imagine you're an explorer navigating through a dense forest. Without a compass, every turn feels uncertain, and you're constantly second-guessing your direction. Your compass during these 50 days is your revision plan. Stick to it, and no matter how overwhelming things get, you'll always find your way back.

Actionable Insight:

- Spend 15 minutes every Sunday refining your revision plan. Treat it as recalibrating your compass for the week ahead.

- Always ask yourself: *"Is this activity bringing me closer to my goal?"*

2. The Phoenix Story: Rising from the Ashes

Every great success story includes failure. Think of the phoenix, which bursts into flames only to rise stronger from its ashes. Similarly, each mock test score, no matter how low, is an opportunity to rebuild yourself with renewed strength.

Student Story:

One of my students, Ananya, once scored 42% in a JEE adv mock test just a month before her exam. Instead of giving up, she analyzed every mistake, turned her weakest subject (Chemistry) into her strongest, and eventually secured an AIR of 524 in JEE Adv.

Quote:

"Our greatest glory is not in never falling, but in rising every time we fall." – Confucius

Actionable Insight:

- Write down three lessons learned from every test. Use them as building blocks for your comeback.

3. The Boulder Metaphor: Keep Pushing

Imagine pushing a massive boulder up a hill. Initially, it feels impossible, but as you persist, it starts to roll. Revision is like that boulder—slow and exhausting at first, but with consistent effort, momentum builds, and the process becomes smoother.

Actionable Insight:

Start each day with 15 minutes of an easy topic to "push

the boulder." This will help you build momentum for tackling tougher concepts later.

4. The Ironman Analogy: Small Wins Lead to Big Victories

In an Ironman triathlon, competitors swim, cycle, and run for hours. Nobody thinks about the entire race all at once. They focus on the next swim stroke, the next pedal, or the next step. Similarly, break your preparation into tiny, manageable tasks.

Quote:

"Success is the sum of small efforts, repeated day in and day out." – Robert Collier

Actionable Insight:

- Write down your tasks for the day on sticky notes. Peel off each note as you complete it, symbolizing progress.

5. The Elephant and the Tiny Mouse Story: Turning Weakness into Strength

In an ancient Indian forest, there was a mighty elephant who ruled the jungle with strength and dominance. One day, the elephant came across a tiny mouse who was meek and small. The elephant laughed at the mouse, mocking its size and power. The mouse, however, was not intimidated. It knew that true strength came from within, not from outward appearances.

Over time, the mouse found ways to outsmart the elephant. It used its agility, cleverness, and understanding of the environment to navigate the challenges the elephant could not. Eventually, the elephant, though strong in size, was humbled by the mouse's persistence and wisdom.

The mouse demonstrated that internal strength—belief in one's capabilities and the courage to act—was more powerful than sheer size or strength. Similarly, in life, even when facing seemingly giant personalities or overwhelming challenges, your inner strength and belief in yourself can help you succeed. It's not the external might that defines you, but the inner courage and determination to rise above. Like David against Goliath in bible, or the mouse against the elephant, the ability to fight against giants lies in the strength you nurture within yourself.

Student Story:

Rohit dreaded Physics, particularly Mechanics. We designed a 7-day micro plan focusing only on basics and previous years' questions. By breaking the "giant" into smaller "pebbles," he aced Mechanics and cleared NEET with ease.

Actionable Insight:

- Identify your "Goliath" topics and divide them into smaller subtopics. Conquer them one at a time.

6. The Candle Flame Metaphor: Protect Your Focus

A single candle can illuminate a dark room, but a gust of wind can easily extinguish it. Your focus is like that flame—precious but fragile. Guard it fiercely.

Quote:

"Starve your distractions, feed your focus."

Actionable Insight:

- Designate a "focus zone" in your study space—free from gadgets and interruptions. Use noise-canceling headphones or soothing instrumental music to create an atmosphere of concentration.

7. The Marathon Story: Pacing Yourself

JEE/NEET/NEET isn't a sprint; it's a marathon. Runners who start too fast often burn out before the finish line. Pacing yourself is the key to lasting till the end with full energy.

Student Story:

Sonia studied for 16 hours daily for a week but felt

exhausted and demotivated by the second week. Switching to a balanced 10-hour study schedule with regular breaks helped her stay consistent and crack NEET with flying colors.

Actionable Insight:

- Follow the **52/17 Rule**: Study for 52 minutes and take a 17-minute break to recharge.

---

8. The Lighthouse Story: Visualize Success

A lighthouse guides ships safely to shore even in the darkest storms. Your goal is that lighthouse—it gives you direction and hope, no matter how rough the journey gets.

Visualization Exercise:

Every night before sleeping, close your eyes and visualize:

- Walking into the exam hall with confidence.
- Solving questions effortlessly.
- Seeing your dream college's name on your admission letter.

Quote:

"Whatever the mind can conceive and believe, it can achieve." – Napoleon Hill

9. The Bamboo Tree Story: Growth Takes Time

Did you know that bamboo trees grow underground for years before sprouting above the surface? But once they start growing, they shoot up to 90 feet in just weeks. Your preparation is like that bamboo tree—results may seem invisible now, but they're coming.

Actionable Insight:

- Track your progress weekly to remind yourself of how far you've come, even if it doesn't feel visible yet.

10. The Archer Metaphor: Aim Steady, Release Confidently

An archer doesn't fire arrows hastily. They take their time, steady their aim, and release with confidence. Similarly, approach each question during practice and exams with a calm, calculated mindset.

Actionable Insight:

- Before starting any test, take three deep breaths to calm your nerves and improve focus.

11. The Bridge Story: Crossing Over to Success

Imagine these last 50 days of preparation, as a bridge that stretches from where you are now to where you want to be—at the threshold of your dreams. This bridge may seem long, and at times, the path might feel shaky or uncertain. But with every small step you take, you get closer to your goal. Each day, as you cross, you strengthen your resolve and build the momentum that will carry you across.

Just like a bridge that withstands the weight of many travellers, these 50 days will help you build your own inner strength, preparing you for the journey ahead. Stay focused, take one step at a time, and trust that each moment of effort brings you closer to the other side—the victory of JEE/NEET and the fulfilment of your dreams.

Quote:

"It always seems impossible until it's done." – Nelson Mandela

Actionable Insight:

- Write a letter to your future self, describing how proud you'll be of your hard work once you've crossed this "bridge."

12. The Mountain Climber's Story:

One Step at a Time

Mountain climbers don't look at the summit constantly- they focus on the next step. Your syllabus is the mountain; take it one chapter, one question, one test at a time.

Student Story:

Ajay struggled with balancing school and JEE prep. By setting daily mini-goals and focusing on incremental progress, he reached his peak—an AIR of 821.

Quote:

"You don't have to see the whole staircase, just take the first step." – Martin Luther King Jr.

Becoming the Legend of Your Story

"You are the protagonist of your story. The obstacles you face today will one day be part of the inspiring tale you tell others. Write this chapter with courage, discipline, and unwavering belief in yourself."

- **Mantra:**

  "I am not defined by my struggles; I am defined by how I overcome them."

CHAPTER 6

Overcoming Exam Hall Nerves: Converting Fear into

Motivation for Achievement

T he exam room can feel like a battlefield, when time constraints, expectations, and anxiety about the future all come together. The familiar faces of your classmates fade into the distance as you enter, and the sound of the clock appears to intensify, enforcing its hold onto your thoughts. Even the most prepared pupils might be overcome by the feelings of self-doubt that seeps in, the dread of failing, and the worry of losing focus. What if, however, you could use this nervousness as a motivating factor to perform with confidence, clarity, and focus?

In order to make every part of your journey—both before and inside the test room—as successful as possible, we'll look at how to turn your exam hall anxiety into a strength in this chapter.

1. Exam Hall Anxiety: The Surge of Nerves

Challenge:

"The moment the paper is in front of me, my heart races, my mind blanks out, and I forget even the simplest concepts."

Story: The Calm River

Think of a river during a storm—it's turbulent, fast, and destructive. But when the storm passes, the river becomes calm and flows smoothly again. Your mind is that river; learning to calm it is the key.

Techniques:

1. **Box Breathing Technique:**

   - Inhale for 4 seconds → Hold for 4 seconds → Exhale for 4 seconds → Hold for 4 seconds. Repeat 3 times. This regulates your heartbeat and calms the mind.

2. **Grounding Exercise:**

   - Place your feet firmly on the floor, feel the pressure, and focus on your breathing. Remind yourself: *"I have prepared for this moment."*

3. **Personal Mantra:**

   - Before the exam, repeat: *"I am calm. I am prepared. I will give my best."*

Case study:

Aparna, a NEET aspirant, struggled with severe anxiety. By practicing breathing techniques for a week before the exam, she reduced her nervousness significantly and completed her paper with confidence.

2. The Fear of Forgetting Concepts

Challenge:

"I studied this chapter yesterday, but now I can't recall anything!"

Story: The Locked Treasure Chest

Your memory is like a treasure chest—it's all there, but the key to unlocking it lies in staying calm and trusting your preparation.

Techniques:

1. **Keyword Recall:**

     o Jot down key formulas, reactions, or concepts in the first 2–3 minutes on the rough sheet. This creates a quick reference for topics you're worried about forgetting.

2. **Pause and Recall:**

     o When you blank out, close your eyes, take a deep breath, and visualize the textbook or notes where you studied the concept.

3. **Memory Trigger Questions:**

   - Ask yourself guiding questions: *"What is this question asking for? What related formula/topic can help here?"*

Case study:

Manoj, a JEE/NEET student, panicked when he forgot a Chemistry formula. By visualizing his notes and linking the question to a related reaction, he recalled the correct answer. This saved him from losing crucial marks.

---

3. Mismanagement of Time

Challenge:

"I run out of time before attempting all the questions."

Story: The Chess Timer

In chess, players allocate time to each move based on its complexity. Similarly, effective time management during exams can make or break your score.

Techniques:

1. **Question Categorization:**

   - **Easy:** Solve these first. Build confidence.

- o **Moderate:** Attempt next; give them a reasonable time.

- o **Difficult:** Save these for last. Avoid spending too much time here. It is so easy to say this, but unless one have a greater command of each chapter-topic-subtopic, it's not possible to categorize. Get command of these points.

2. **Time Tracking:**

   - o Divide the total time into sections. E.g., for a 3-hour paper:

     - 1st hour: Solve all easy questions.

     - 2nd hour: Focus on moderate ones.

     - 3rd hour: Attempt the difficult ones or review answers.

3. **Skip-and-Return Rule:**

   - o If a question takes more than 90 seconds and you're unsure, mark it to revisit later.

Case study:

Rajesh, a JEE/NEET aspirant, used to get stuck on Physics numericals. By skipping time-consuming questions and revisiting them in the last 30 minutes, he attempted 95% of the paper efficiently.

---

4. Negative Marking Pressure

Challenge:

"I'm scared of making mistakes and losing marks due to negative marking."

Story: The Archer and the Target

An archer doesn't shoot blindly at the target—they calculate the angle and aim with precision. In exams, accuracy is more important than speed to avoid unnecessary penalties.

Techniques:

1. **50:50 Elimination Rule:**

   - If unsure, eliminate two incorrect options first. Only attempt if confident about the remaining two options. In JEE/NEET, better leave if you are unsure. This method work in state wise entrance exams or less tough exams.

2. **Bookmark Strategy:**

   o   If a question seems too risky, bookmark it and return it only if you have extra time.

3. **Trust Your Gut:**

   o   Research suggests your first instinct is often correct. Don't overthink once you've chosen an answer.

Case study:

Neha, a NEET student, lost marks in her mocks due to over-attempting. She learned to attempt only when 70% confident and improved her accuracy, boosting her overall score.

5. Unclear Questions and Overthinking

Challenge:

"Sometimes, questions seem tricky, and I spend too much time decoding them".

Story: The Foggy Windshield

When driving in fog, you slow down and focus carefully on the road ahead. Similarly, for tricky questions, slowing down and simplifying can help you see the "road" clearly.

Techniques:

1. **Rephrase the Question:**

   o   Simplify it in your own words. Ask: *"What is the examiner really testing here?"*

2. **Highlight Key Words:**

   o   Underline important terms in the question (e.g., NOT, ALWAYS, MAXIMUM). This avoids misinterpretation.

3. **Break It Down:**

   o   Divide complex problems into smaller parts. Solve step by step rather than trying to do it all at once.

Case study:

Kriti often misunderstood Biology MCQs. By underlining key words and rephrasing questions, she improved her accuracy significantly in the final NEET exam.

6. Getting Stuck on One Question

Challenge:

"I waste too much time on a single question, and it throws off my rhythm."

Story: The Sinking Boat

If a boat starts sinking, you don't stay and fix it—you move to another boat to survive. Similarly, if a question feels like a "sinking boat," move on to save your time.

Techniques:

1. **2-Minute Rule:**

   o   If you're stuck for more than 2 minutes, skip the question and come back later.

2. **Quick Guess:**

   o   If partially confident, take an educated guess and mark it.

3. **Prioritize Flow:**

   o   Maintain momentum by solving familiar questions first. This builds confidence for harder ones.

Case study:

Ramesh struggled with long Physics calculations. By using the 2-minute rule, he completed 95% of his paper, leaving time to revisit tough questions.

---

7. Losing Focus Mid-Exam

Challenge:

"I start strong, but halfway through the paper, I lose concentration."

Story: The Marathon Runner

Marathon runners refuel with energy drinks and pace themselves to stay consistent throughout the race. Similarly, you need to "refuel" your focus during exams.

Techniques:

1. **Micro-Breaks:**

   - Every 45 minutes, take a 10-second break. Close your eyes, breathe deeply, and stretch your fingers.

2. **Pep Talk:**

Mentally say: *"Halfway done! Keep going strong."*

3. **Reset Posture:**

   - Sit upright, relax your shoulders, and adjust your grip on the pen. A physical reset helps refresh the mind.

Case study:

Sanya, a NEET student, struggled with mid-exam fatigue. By practicing micro-breaks during mocks, she maintained focus and completed her paper without losing steam.

---

8. Feeling Overwhelmed by the Clock

Challenge:

"The ticking clock makes me panic and rush through questions."

Story: The Hourglass

An hourglass doesn't let all the sand fall at once—it allows a steady flow. Similarly, instead of rushing through the exam, pace yourself steadily.

Techniques:

1. **Divide Time:**

   - Allocate time for each section (e.g., 1 hour for Physics,

1 hour for Chemistry, 1 hour for Math/Biology). Stick to these boundaries.

2. **Time Checks:**

   o Every 30 minutes, glance at the clock to ensure you're on track. Avoid constant clock-watching.

3. **Positive Clock View:**

   o Instead of seeing the clock as a threat, view it as a guide keeping you disciplined.

The Game-Changer-1: Water – Your Secret to Exam Success

In the examination hall, it's natural for most students to feel anxious and experience mental fatigue after some time. While it might seem like there's little you can do in that moment, the secret weapon is surprisingly simple—**water**. Yes, water can be a game-changer for your brain!

Sadly, some students deliberately reduce their water intake during exams to avoid the inconvenience of visiting the washroom. This habit can backfire, as even mild dehydration reduces focus and increases fatigue. The *British Journal of Nutrition* (2013) found that dehydration significantly affects memory, attention, and mood—critical factors in exam performance.

Meanwhile, research from the *International Journal of Environmental Research and Public Health* (2019) showed that rehydration reduces mental fatigue and improves reaction time and short-term memory. A study by Benton and Burgess (2009) revealed that students who sipped water during exams performed up to **10% better** than those who didn't.

So, the solution is simple: **bring a water bottle into your exams and sip regularly**. Don't sacrifice your brain's power for the fear of needing a break. Taking small sips is enough to keep your mind fresh and sharp. Next time you feel stressed, or your thoughts get cloudy, take a sip—it's your brain's reset button!

Here's a graphical representation of **student efficiency in the exam hall over time**:

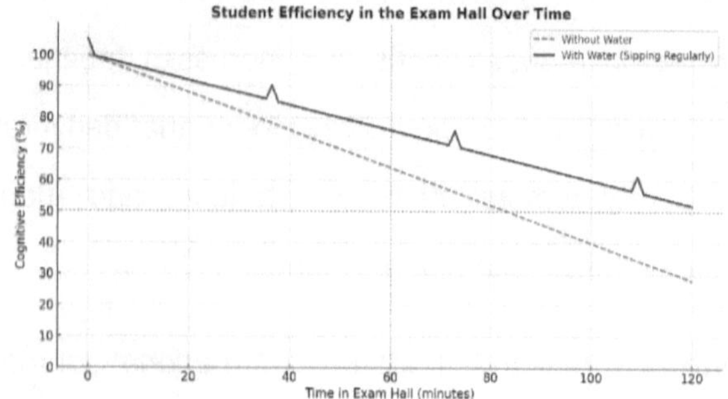

Dotted Line (Without Water): Efficiency drops steadily, reaching below 50% after 60 minutes due to mental fatigue and dehydration.

Continuous Line (With Regular Water Sipping): Efficiency declines more slowly, with noticeable boosts every 30 minutes after drinking water, helping students stay focused and sharp.

This visual demonstrates how something as simple as sipping water can significantly impact.

The Game-Changer-2: Simple Breathing Techniques – Overcoming Exam Hall Anxiety

In the examination hall, the majority of students often experience mental blocks, making it difficult to recall and apply their knowledge effectively after some time. **Here, time is more precious, and coming out of this state**

quickly is essential for success. Then what can be done to turn it around? At the same time, movement is restricted, and every second counts—yet there is a **boon** that can help: **controlled breathing.**

Scientific studies prove that mindful breathing techniques can instantly stabilize stress levels and enhance cognitive clarity. A study published in *Frontiers in Psychology* confirms that **deep, structured breathing reduces test anxiety and sharpens mental focus**, enabling students to regain control in critical moments (Frontiers Study). Likewise, research from *PMC* highlights how **breathwork regulates stress responses, optimizes energy, and improves cognitive performance**, preventing students from feeling drained and overwhelmed (PMC Study). A simple **30-second breathing exercise**—inhaling deeply for four counts, holding for four counts, and exhaling for six counts—can **reset the mind, restore confidence, and prevent costly mental fatigue. Neglecting this technique can leave students struggling under pressure, limiting their ability to perform at their best and seize future opportunities.** Mastering this small yet powerful method can be the key to unlocking true potential when it matters the most.

(https://www.frontiersin.org/journals/psycholog y/articles/10.3389/fpsyg.2022.678098/full

https://pmc.ncbi.nlm.nih.gov/articles/PMC987 3947/)

The Warrior's Calm

In ancient battles, warriors entered the battlefield with unwavering focus, their minds calm yet sharp. The exam hall is your battlefield. Stay calm, trust your preparation, and strike with precision.

Quote:

"A calm mind brings inner strength and self-confidence, so that's very important for good health." – Dalai Lama

Final Reminder:

"The exam is not the end of your journey—it's a steppingstone. Stay calm, stay focused, and give it your best. Your preparation has prepared you for this moment."

Conclusion: The Journey Ahead – Your Future Awaits

As you reach the end of this journey through the pages of this book, remember that the road to success is not defined by how quickly you reach the finish line, but by the persistence, resilience, and determination you show along the way. The challenges you face in JEE/NEET preparation—whether it's managing your time, battling distractions, overcoming self-doubt, or mastering subjects that seem impossible—are not obstacles; they are opportunities in disguise. Each struggle you overcome adds strength to your foundation, shaping you not just for this exam, but for the greater challenges life will present. You have the power to transform anxiety into action, procrastination into productivity, and self-doubt into unshakable confidence. The journey may seem tough at times, but with the right mindset, the strategies shared in this book, and your own unwavering commitment, you are more than capable of turning your aspirations into achievements.

As you move forward, take these lessons with you: **trust in your preparation, believe in your growth, and embrace every step of the journey with confidence that you are ready.** Every day of study, every challenge faced, and every small win brings you closer to the success you deserve. And remember, this exam is just one chapter in your story—your future is filled with limitless possibilities, and this experience will only make you stronger, wiser, and more prepared for whatever lies ahead.

The journey toward your dreams has only just begun. Step forward with hope, determination, and the belief that you are capable of achieving greatness. Your future awaits, and it is brighter than you can imagine.

"At last, the ultimate success formula for JEE/NEET—where creativity meets relentless hard work, and strong focus lasts long stretches of dedication. This is the path of the unstoppable!"

Go forward with hope, determination, and a heart full of belief. **Best wishes for your success—may you shine bright and achieve everything you've dreamed of!**

Best wishes!

N.B.V.SubbaRao,

"I am your companion in every hurdle you face, believing wholeheartedly in your success".

A Heartfelt Note from the Author

Your success is the true purpose of these pages; I'd be humbled to hear how it's helped you and love to celebrate together. I'm just a call or email away.

"Innovating Education with Mindset & Practical Solutions for Parents, Teachers, and Students"

www.ingramcontent.com/pod-product-compliance
Lightning Source LLC
Chambersburg PA
CBHW021232130726
47988CB00002B/935